JAM JAM JAM

with
BRIAN SETZER

TOTAL ACCURACY
IMP
Professional Guitar Workshops

CONTENTS

ON THE CD

The CD is split into two sections; section 1 (tracks 1-8) is the backing tracks minus lead guitar & vocals, while section 2 (tracks 9-16) is the backing tracks with all guitar parts added, so in addition to the written tab you can hear the rhythm, fills and solos as they should be played!!

WARNER BROS. PUBLICATIONS - THE GLOBAL LEADER IN PRINT
USA: 15800 NW 48th Avenue, Miami, FL33014

WARNER/CHAPPELL MUSIC

CANADA: 85 SCARSDALE ROAD, SUITE 101
DON MILLS, ONTARIO, M3B 2R2
SCANDINAVIA: PO BOX 533, VENDEVAGEN 85 B
S-182 15 DANDERYD, SWEDEN
AUSTRALIA: PO BOX 353
3 TALAVERA ROAD, NORTH RYDE N.S.W. 2113

NUOVA CARISCH

ITALY: VIA CAMPANIA, 12
20098 SAN GIULIANO
MILANESE - MILANO
SPAIN: MAGALLANES, 25
28015 MADRID

INTERNATIONAL MUSIC PUBLICATIONS LIMITED

ENGLAND: SOUTHEND ROAD
WOODFORD GREEN, ESSEX IG8 8HN
FRANCE: 25 RUE D'HAUTEVILLE, 75010 PARIS
GERMANY: MARSTALLSTR. 8, D-80539 MUNCHEN
DENMARK: DANMUSIK, VOGNMAGERGADE 7
DK 1120 KOBENHAVNK

First Edition 1997
© 1997 International Music Publications Limited
Southend Road, Woodford Green, Essex IG8 8HN, England
All rights reserved

Music arranged & produced by Stuart Bull and Steve Finch. Recorded at the TOTAL ACCURACY SOUNDHOUSE, Romford, England.
Steve Finch: drums, Richard Barrett: guitar, Mick Ash: bass. Music engraving: Chris Francis

Professional Guitar Workshops

Introduction

The TOTAL ACCURACY 'JAM WITH...' series, is a powerful learning tool that will help you extend your stockpile of licks and fills and develop your improvisational skills. The combination of musical notation and guitar tablature in the book together with backing tracks on the CD gives you the opportunity to learn each track note for note and then jam with a professional session band. The track listing reflects some of Brian Setzer's most popular recordings, providing something for guitarists to have fun with and improvise with, as well as something to aspire to.

The first eight tracks on the CD are full length backing tracks recorded minus lead guitar. The remaining tracks feature the backing tracks with the lead guitar parts added. Although many of you will have all the original tracks in your own collection, we have provided them in the package for your reference. The 'JAM WITH...' series allows you to accurately recreate the original, or to use the transcriptions in this book in conjunction with the backing tracks as a basis for your own improvisation. For your benefit we have put definite endings on the backing tracks, rather than fading these out as is the case on some of the original recordings. The accompanying transcriptions correspond to our versions. Remember, experimenting with your own ideas is equally important for developing your own style; most important of all however is that you enjoy JAM with BRIAN SETZER and HAVE FUN!

In the early '80s, The Stray Cats enjoyed a meteoric rise to fame in a short but intense period of chart success. Their infectious rockabilly sound was instantly recognizable, as were the band themselves. They had an upright double-bass player, a drummer who stood up and a front man who had the most elaborate quiff seen since the '50s.

The Stray Cats were made up of three former New York school friends, Lee Rocker (bass), Slim Jim Phantom (drums) and Brian Setzer (guitar & vocals). Brian was also playing with another band, The Bloodless Pharoahs, but when they split he focused his attention on The Stray Cats and the writing of their own traditionally styled new material. His biggest influence was Eddie Cochran, from his personal style to the guitar - the synonymous 1959 Gretsch 6120 which amongst others he still uses today.

In July 1980 the band and Tony Bidgood, their manager, moved to the U.K. with the promise of some gigs, only to find on arrival that the gigs and the accommodation were 'unavailable'! Undeterred, they persisted in getting themselves on the London club circuit where their well received performances quickly attracted good music press coverage and record company interest. So good in fact, that just eight weeks after these three unknowns moved to England, they opened for Elvis Costello at The Rainbow in Finsbury Park.

The following month they were signed to Arista Records and in December their debut single "Runaway Boys" reached No. 9. In February the following year, "Rock This Town" reached the same position and their eponymous debut album reached No. 6 in March. "Stray Cat Strut", probably the bands most famous track, followed and reached No.11. The remainder of 1981 was mainly spent touring, selling out in the U.K., Europe and Australia and also supporting The Rolling Stones in the States.

In 1982 the band were finally signed in the U.S.A. and undertook a three month tour to try and ensure success in their own country, which had so far eluded them. A compilation of their earlier U.K. albums, "Built For Speed" was released for the U.S. and stayed at No.2 for fifteen weeks, held off firstly by Men At Work and then by Michael Jackson. It still sold over 2 million copies and earned the band a platinum disc.

In August of the following year, The Stray Cats achieved their last U.K. hit with "(She's) Sexy And 17". The third album, "Rant 'N' Rave With The Stray Cats" peaked at No. 51 and after further success in the U.S., The Stray Cats decided to split in February 1984 with Brian going on to pursue a solo career. Slim Jim Phantom married the actress Britt Ekland on his 23rd birthday and along with Lee Rocker and David Bowie's ex-guitarist formed a new band imaginatively called Phantom, Rocker and Slick.

After two solo albums and a role in the Ritchie Valens biopic movie "La Bamba" playing his hero Eddie Cochran, Brian and the guys reunited for a 35 date U.S. tour and some recording sessions with original producer Dave Edmunds. The reunion album "Blast Off" was released but did not make any serious chart presence.

Today, Brian has diversified. He fronts the 17 piece Brian Setzer Orchestra and has now released two albums incorporating the big band sound with serious lead guitar.

Brian Setzer is now a highly respected guitarist with his own highly influenced style and "Jam With Brian Setzer" documents his best known early compositions as well as the tracks that The Stray Cats amongst others, made famous.

Performance Notes

Rock This Town

The intro of this track is played on unaccompanied guitar, strumming a swing rhythm on a D major chord. After four bars of this, the upright bass and drums join in and the guitar part soon changes to a chunky, palm muted figure with a Chuck Berry type feel. The whole song is built around a standard 12-bar chord progression using D major, G major and A major. There are several variations on these chords as the song progresses, such as D9, D69, E6, and E7. These variations come into play mostly in the bridge and chorus sections, where Brian is using a more jazzy, less muted 'comping' style.

The solo work has a very traditional rockabilly feel, using the D minor pentatonic scale (D,F,G,A,C). Lots of double stop licks, slides and bluesy quarter tone bends add to the overall effect. Perhaps the most authentic sounding part of the solo happens in bars 75/76, where there is a double stop phrase using the notes F natural and B together, giving an augmented 4th/diminished 5th interval, a popular rock and roll trick.

Finally, the last two bars of the solo are played using the B minor pentatonic scale - the relative minor key-then segueing back into the main verse riff. The final verse, chorus and outro show Brian expanding on the idea of adding solo phrases between vocal lines, making them more frequent and experimental. The song finishes with a run using the D minor pentatonic scale. concluding with a D69 chord which is dipped slightly below pitch then returned, using the tremelo. This track was played on a Gretsch 6120 or White Falcon through Fender amps.

Stray Cat Strut

The upright bass and drums introduce this song coming to a dead stop after the second bar, where the guitar plays an unaccompanied two bar solo fill, using the C minor pentatonic scale (C, Eb, F, G,Bb). During the second of this, the choice of notes is unusual, including B natural, Db and A natural, all from outside the parent scale, almost giving the effect of a brief key change, before returning to the original key for the verse, once again with the whole band, playing a descending chord progression of C minor, Bb7, Ab7 and G7, using the root note in octaves at first, introducing the full chords. Occasionally, variants of these chords are used as the song progresses eg; Bb6, Ab6 and a bridge section using F minor, F min9 and the very jazzy sounding Gb9b13.

The first solo kicks off in a swing style, almost reminiscent of Django Reinhardt - especially during bar 42. Continuing on this jazzy theme, there is a descending series of fragmented chords in bars 45/46, followed by an ascending run using slides and a 'whole tone' scale effect, neatly joining up with the bridge via a series of double stops. Here, there is another verse, which is then repeated instrumentally, using a more 'jazz' comping style, incorporating a G augmented 7th chord, which adds tension.

The second solo is similar in style and content to the first, though uses more tremelo and a couple of downward 'raked' lines. After the final bridge and verse, there is a short fill using the C minor pentatonic, incorporating A and B natural. Finally, a C minor 69 chord is quickly alternate strummed in free time, bringing this track to a dramatic close. This track was played on a Gretsch 6120 or White Falcon through Fender amps.

Runaway Boys

This track is built around a descending bass riff in the key of E, straddling the gap between major and minor, but using C#, from the E major scale and a G natural, from the E minor scale. From bar 5, the key changes to F# major, featuring a series of double stop licks on the guitar. After a short burst of rhythmic 'stabs', the key shifts back to E and a ringing E minor chord which is lowered in pitch using the tremelo. The verse uses the descending bass line again, shifting to A5 then C5 chords in the bridge, which build all the way through until it reaches a crescendo with another ringing E minor chord and subsequent verse. After the following chorus, there is a section in F#, similar to the intro, but this time with the vocal following the melody line previously played on the guitar in double stops and the guitar playing chunky, semi-palm muted chord backing.

The solo kicks in dramatically using fast pull-offs in the first position of the E blues scale (E,G,A,Bb,B,D). It continues using this position until bar 67, when the same scale is used 12 frets/one octave higher. In bar 71 it shifts back again, culminating with some tremelo work on the open low E string. This is followed shortly after by a repeat of the intro double stop section, in a similar arrangement to it's first appearance. After a repeat of the first verse, this section is repeated again, though using the version which appears just before the solo. After a slightly extended chorus, the song comes to an abrupt finish during the bassline/main riff. This track was played on a Gretsch 6120 or White Falcon through Fender amps.

(She's) Sexy And 17

This track is played in the key of E, with a capo at the first fret, so it actually sounds in the key of F. To make the guitar notation easier to read, it is written in the key of E, as it is played.

The first riff is based around the low register of the E blues scale (E,G,A,Bb,B,D) - substituting a G sharp in place of the usual G. After the first four bars, this is punctuated with chord 'stabs', which are slid down the fretboard, The song is built around a standard 12-bar type chord progression, with the riff following E,A and B chords. Other chord embellishments, along with the previously mentioned 'stabs', include E9, E7, E6, A9, A7 and B7. During the verses, the guitar solo begins with some triplet pull-off phrases, using notes from the high register of the first position E blues scale.

It continues in this style, working down into the lower register, until bar 93, when the blues scale shifts up to the third position, though still incorporating open strings. Briefly, it shifts back to the first position, using a generic augmented 4th/diminished 5th interval - C# and G natural together - then up an octave for two bars, followed by a series of slides down the G string, leading out of the solo into a bridge-type section in A. This leads back into the final verse and chorus, ending on an F69 followed by an E69 chord, which is left to ring. This track was played on a Gretsch 6120 or White Falcon through Fender amps.

Rumble In Brighton

This track bursts into life with a B7#9 chord, using hard alternate strumming with a triplet feel. This is followed by an E minor chord, which is left to ring over a riff played on the bass and guitar, using the E minor pentatonic scale (E,G,A,B,D). During this section, the same effect is achieved using an A minor chord and the A minor pentatonic scale (A,C,D,E,G). There is also some use of power chords, played in a semi palm muted style, incorporating an alternating bass line, giving this section it's 'minor' feel.

It becomes apparent here that the guitar tone used is slightly more distorted than on the other tracks. However, this effect is still quite subtle and is probably a result of sheer volume. After this ascending riff has built to a crescendo, the first verse begins, based around a 12-bar type chord progression using E minor, A minor and B minor. After the first chorus the intro is repeated in full, leading to the second verse and chorus. The solo begins here, using the E blues scale (E,G,A,Bb,B,D) - with a series of hammer-ons on the B and G strings, alternating with open notes on the high E and B strings. In bar 89, Brian shifts down to the first position of this scale, then plays a series of pull-offs across all six strings. At bar 94, A minor and B minor chord patterns are played at the 12th and 14th frets respectively, in a similar style to the chorus, leading to a final E minor chord, which is played through an electronic tremelo effect.

From here, the ascending riff from the intro leads into the final verse, which is played in a similar manner to all the preceding verses. However, the last chorus is heavily embellished with fills taken from the E blues scale and one from the A blues scale (A,C,D,Eb,G) at bar 136/7. The song draws to a close with two chords strummed once in free time, an E minor and an E minor add 9, once again giving the ending a touch of drama. This track was played on a Gretsch 6120 or White Falcon through Fender amps.

Fishnet Stockings

Beginning with an A chord on the first beat of each bar, in classic rock'n'roll style, this up-tempo track uses the standard 12-bar chord progression, featuring A,A5,A6,D9,E and E6 chords. Apart from the first line of each verse, the chord work is played in a loose fingerstyle pattern, outlining the chords without becoming too intricate or full sounding.

The first guitar solo begins with an attention grabbing series of double stops during the first six bars, at bar 34 featuring the augmented 4th/diminished 5th interval which characterises much of Brian's solo work. This leads directly to a series of phrases using the A blues scale (A,C,D,Eb,E,G). In bars 36 and 37, a repetitive 'raked' pattern is played along with the bluesy idea of bending the minor 3rd (in this case C) up a quarter tone. Bars 44/5 show a triplet based pull-off pattern segueing into a Chuck Berry style rock'n'roll lick, then some jazz style passing note phrases finish this solo off at bars 49 to 52. A further verse and chorus follow, leading straight to a second guitar solo, beginning with a pull-off phrase which 'pivots' off an F sharp - as would feature in an A6 chord. In this solo, Brian pulls out all the stops, using fast repetitive phrasing, double stops and vamping on some jazzy chord fragments to bring this solo to a close. After the final verse and chorus, the song ends with a held A6 chord, which is modulated slightly with the tremelo. This track was played on a Gretsch 6120 or White Falcon through Fender amps.

Double-Talkin' Baby

Again, an up tempo track in the key of A, beginning in true rock'n'roll style with a guitar figure incorporating the classic sounding augmented 4th/diminished 5th interval, bent a quarter tone sharp for a bluesy effect. The standard 12-bar shuffle feel of the verse is punctuated by jazzy chord stabs from Brian using mainly 9 and 69 chords. The last part of the progression has a stop-start feel, moving chromatically up and down the same 7th chord shape, between the D and E. During the next section, there is a twist to the theme, adding an extra of A69 at bar 23. This does not alter the time signature, but shifts the rhythmic emphasis of the chord changes. The first guitar solo uses the A blues scale (A,C,D,Eb,E,G) incorporating all Brian's favourite bend and double stop tricks, staying mainly in the first position of the scale. After the next verse and chorus, the second solo follows similar lines, though is more flash, using fast pull-offs, wide string bends, heavy vibrato and occasional staccato phrasing.

From bar 103, Brian uses a chord 'vamping' technique, sliding the usual chords up an octave then sliding down the chord shape using fast tremelo picking at bar 106. From here, the rest of the solo is played mostly in the first position of the scale again, leading to the final verse and chorus, ending the track with a solo phrase similar to the intro and an A69 chord. This track was played on a Gretsch 6120 or White Falcon through Fender amps.

Built For Speed

With chord backing played throughout on acoustic guitar, this track features a double stop pattern on the lead guitar, alternating with loose fingerstyle picking around the main chords of E,A and B major. After the second verse and chorus, the guitar solo begins with a fast tremelo picked 69 chord shape, slid up the fretboard. This shape provides the basis of the solo, with a few alternating bass notes, until bar 89 when it changes to a more blues scale based idea in E (E,G,A,Bb,D), shifting notes down chromatically against an E 'pivot'.

The descending chromatic theme continues with a double stop pattern in bar 92, alternating between this type of idea and standard blues scale phrases until bar 98, when the solo winds up with a shuffle bass line played in the lower register. The final verse and chorus follow the same pattern as their predecessors and the track finishes, after a short outro, with a held E69 chord. This track was played on a Gretsch 6120 or White Falcon through Fender amps.

Notation & Tablature explained

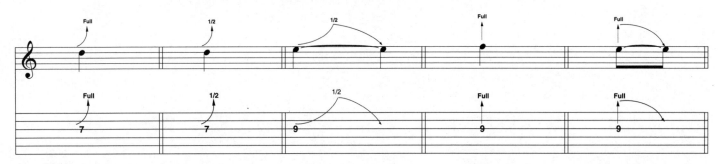

BEND: Strike the note
and bend up a whole step
(two frets)

BEND: Strike the note
and bend up a half step
(one fret)

BEND AND RELEASE: Strike
the note, bend up a half step,
then release the bend.

PRE-BEND: Bend the
note up, then strike it

PRE-BEND AND RELEASE:
Bend up, strike the note,
then release it

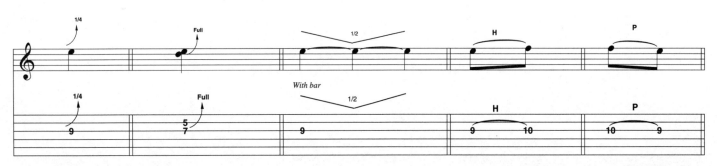

QUARTER-TONE BEND:
Bend the note slightly
sharp

UNISON BEND: Strike both
notes, then bend the lower
note up to the pitch of the
higher one

TREMOLO BAR BENDS: Strike the
note, and push the bar down and up
by the amounts indicated

HAMMER-ON: Strike the first
note, then sound the second
by fretting it without picking

PULL-OFF: Strike the higher
note, then pull the finger off
while keeping the lower
one fretted

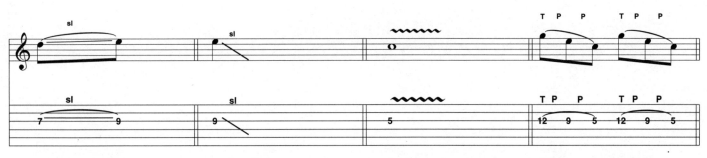

SLIDE: Slide the finger
from the first note to
the second. Only the
first note is struck

SLIDE: Slide to the fret
from a few frets below or
above

VIBRATO: The string is vibrated
by rapidly bending and releasing
a note with the fretboard hand
or tremolo bar

TAPPING: Hammer on to the
note marked with a T using the
picking hand, then pull off to
the next note, following the
hammer-ons or pull-offs in the
normal way

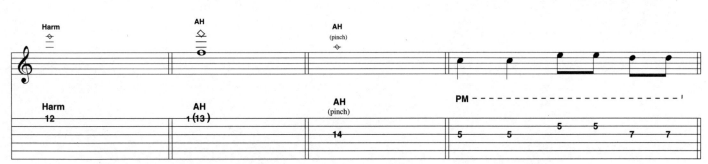

NATURAL HARMONIC:
Lightly touch the string directly
over the fret shown, then strike
the note to create a "chiming"
effect

ARTIFICIAL HARMONIC:
Fret the note, then use the
picking hand finger to touch
the string at the position
shown in brackets and pluck
with another finger

ARTIFICIAL HARMONIC:
The harmonic is produced
by using the edge of the
picking hand thumb to
"pinch" the string whilst
picking firmly with
the plectrum

PALM MUTES: Rest the
palm of the picking hand
on the strings near the bridge to
produce a muted effect. Palm
mutes can apply to a single note
or a number of notes
(shown with a dashed line)

Rock This Town

Words and Music by BRIAN SETZER

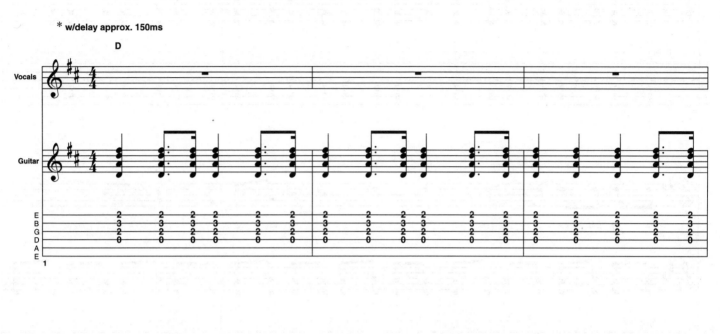

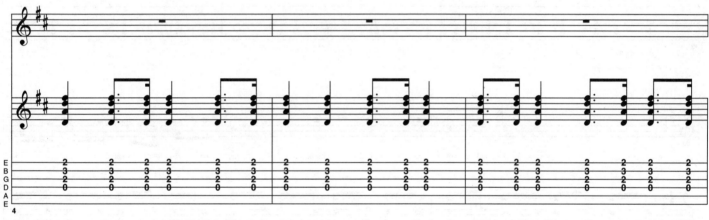

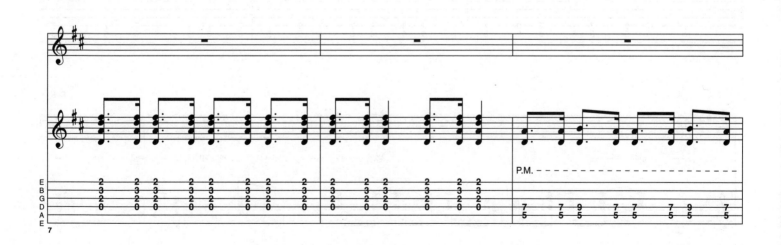

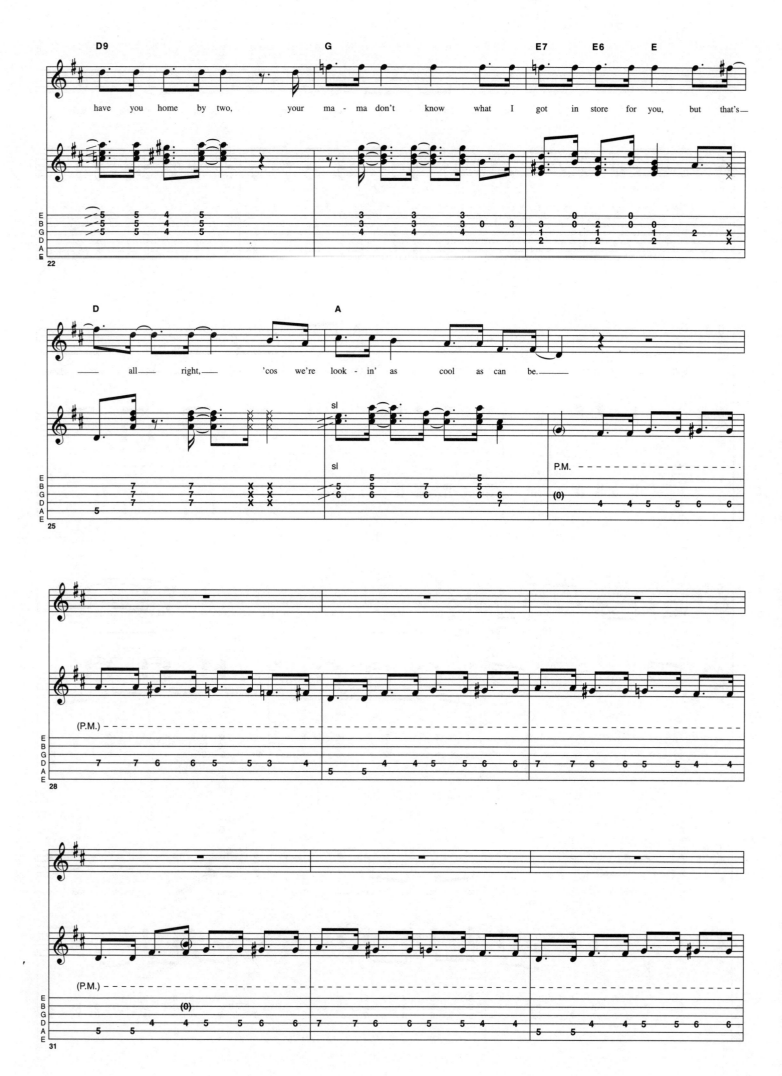

have you home by two, your ma-ma don't know what I got in store for you, but that's— all— right,— 'cos we're look-in' as cool as can be.—

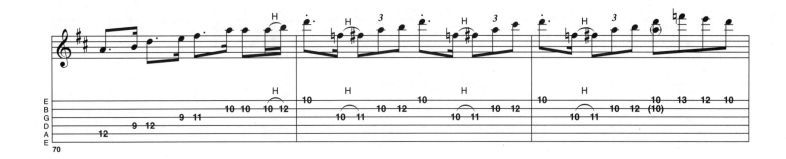

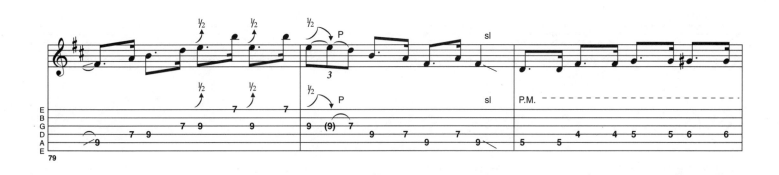

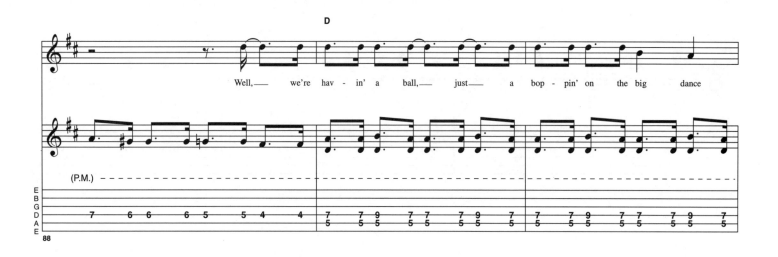

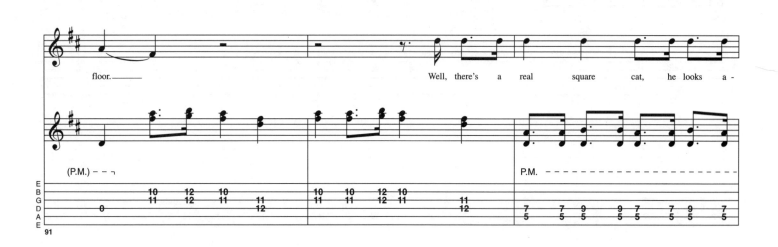

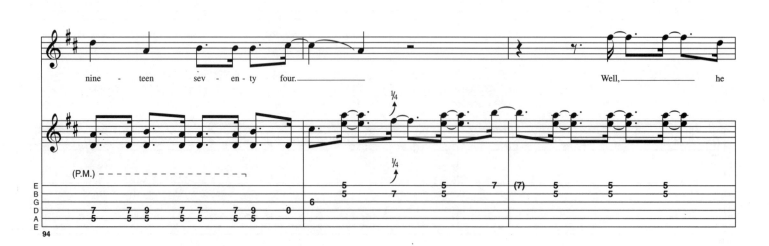

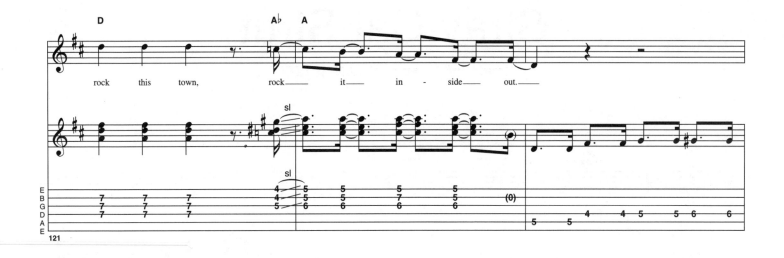

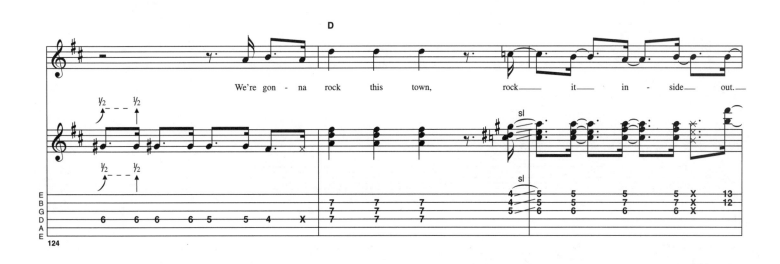

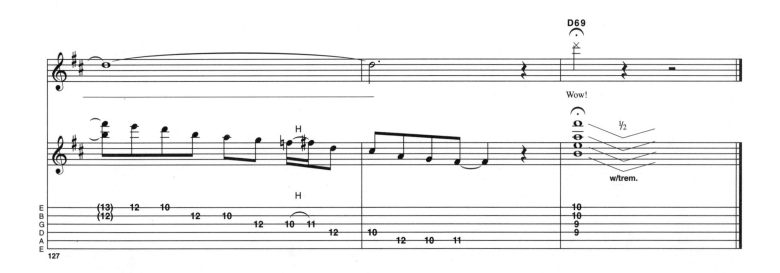

Stray Cat Strut

Words and Music by BRIAN SETZER

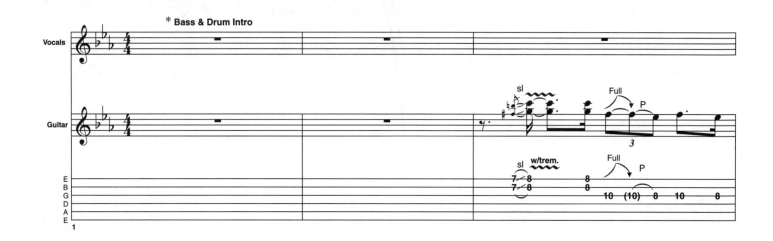

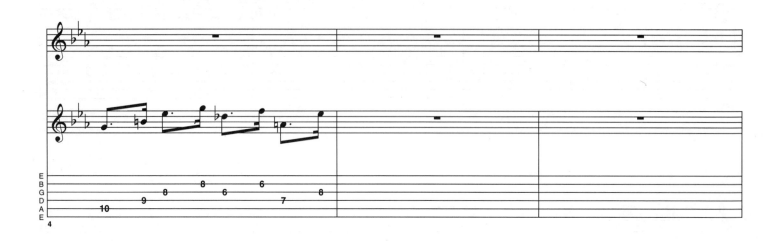

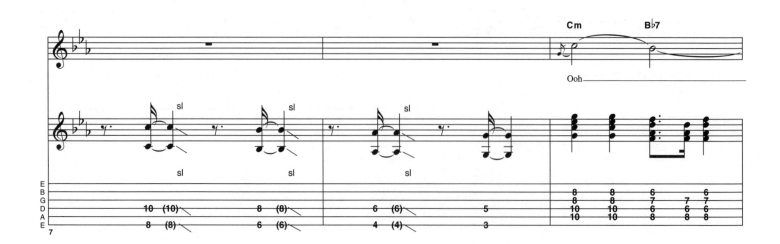

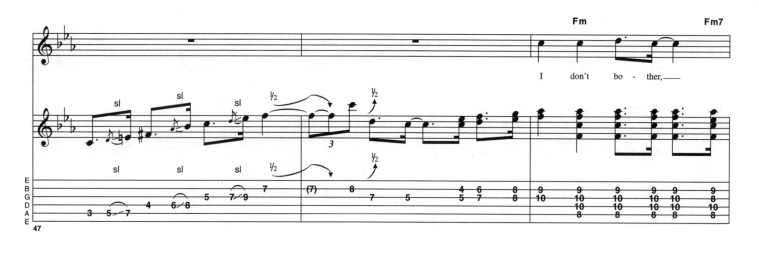

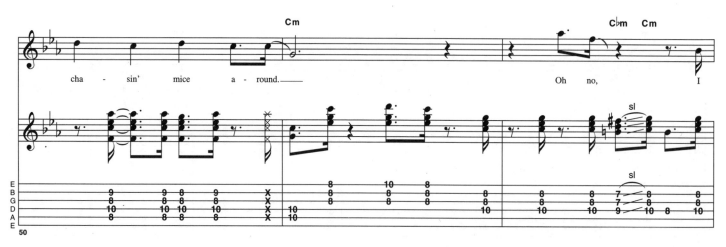

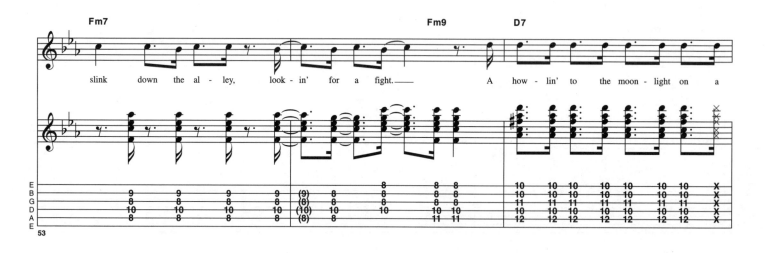

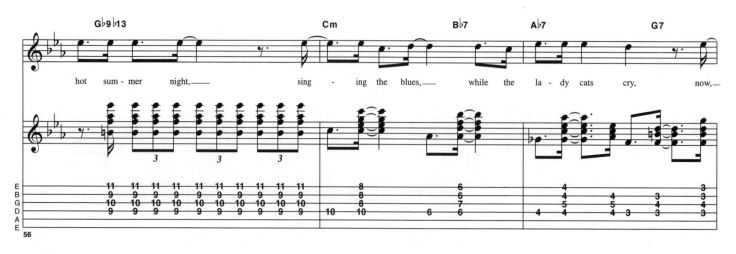

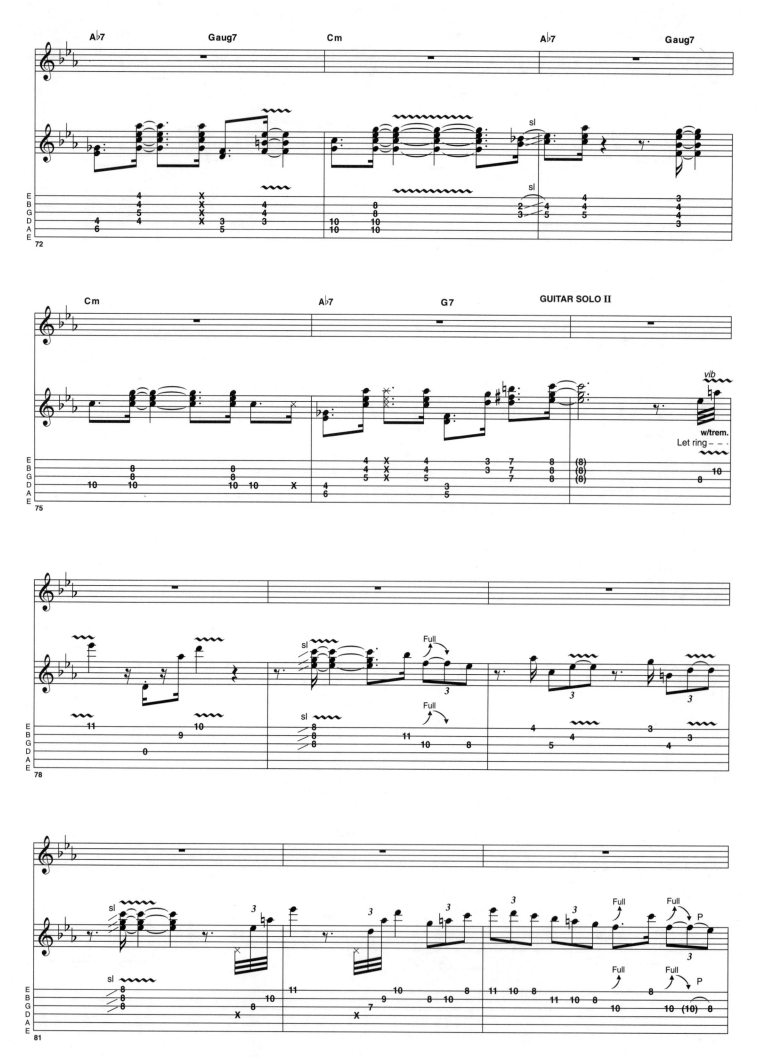

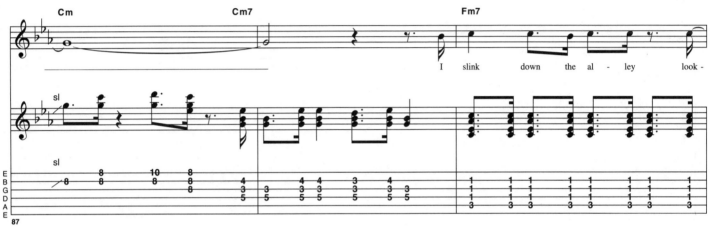

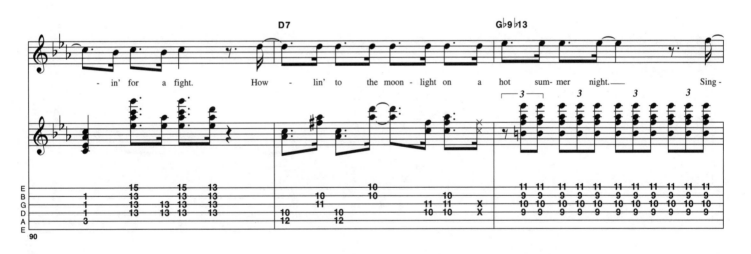

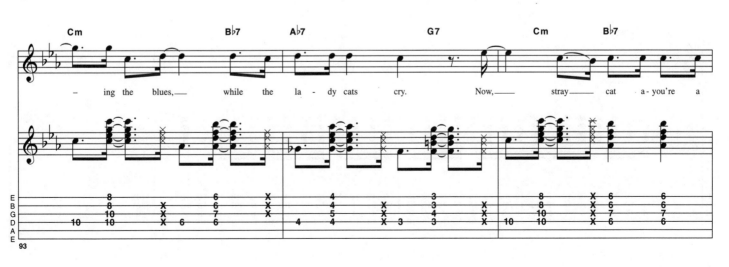

Runaway Boys

Words and Music by BRIAN SETZER,
SLIM JIM PHANTOM and LEE ROCKER

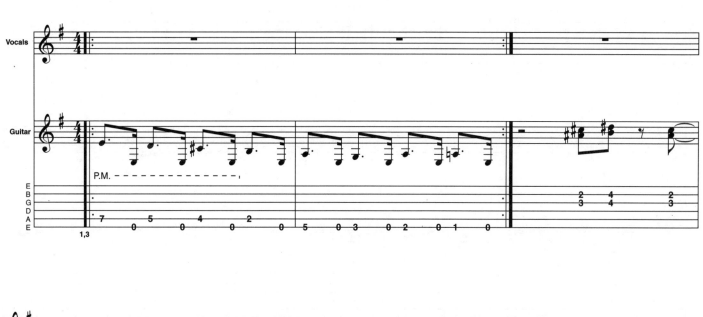

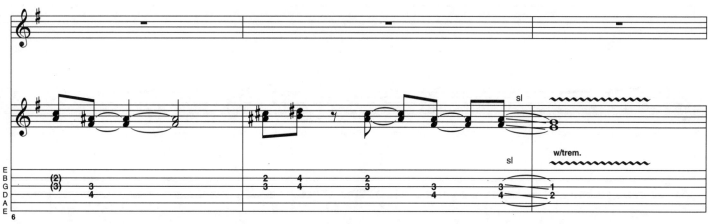

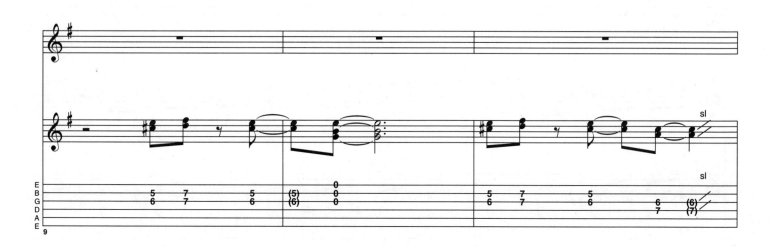

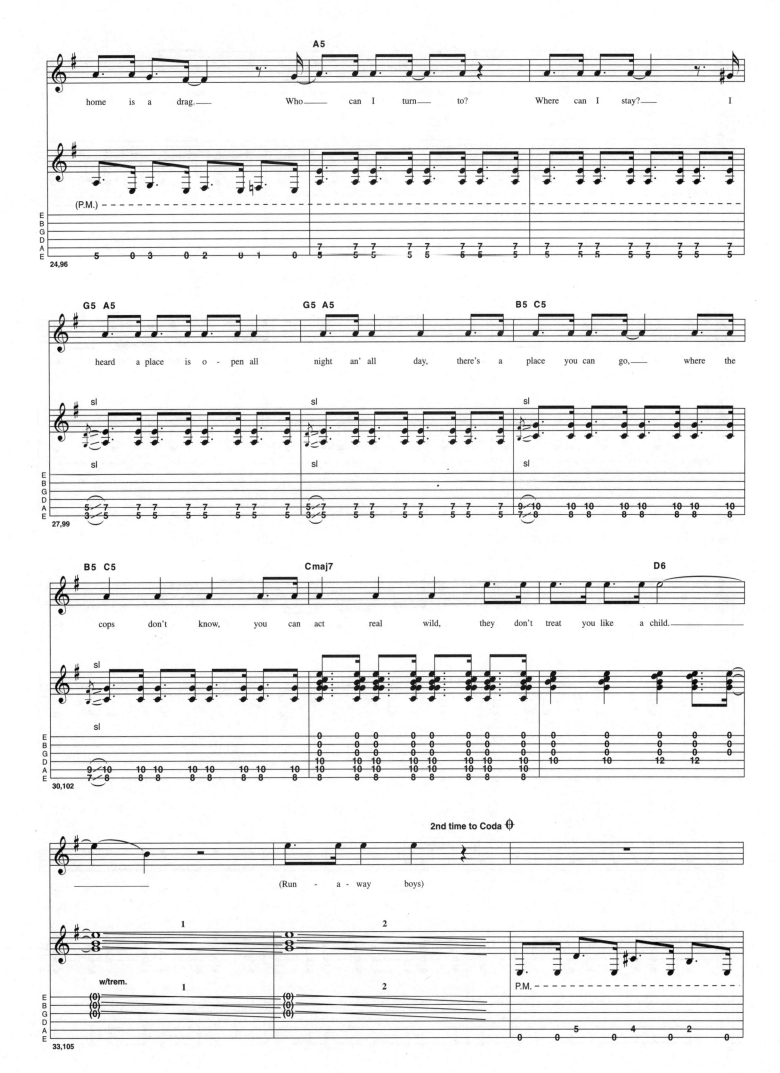

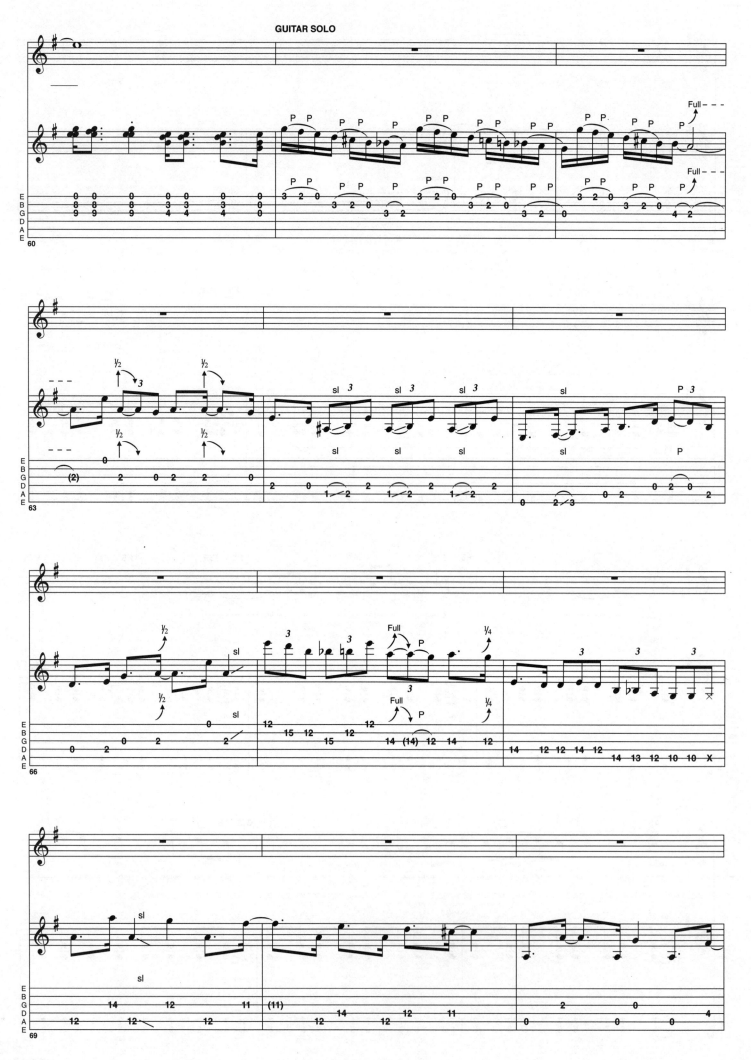

(She's) Sexy And 17

Words and Music by BRIAN SETZER

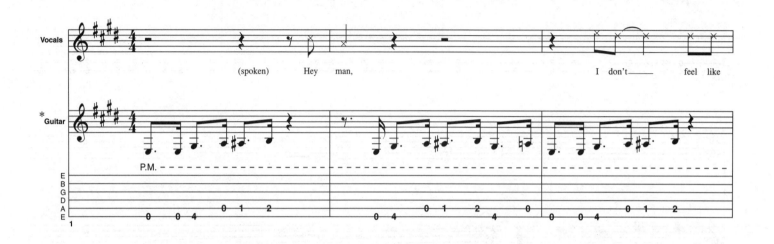

Rumble In Brighton

Words and Music by BRIAN SETZER,
SLIM JIM PHANTOM and LEE ROCKER

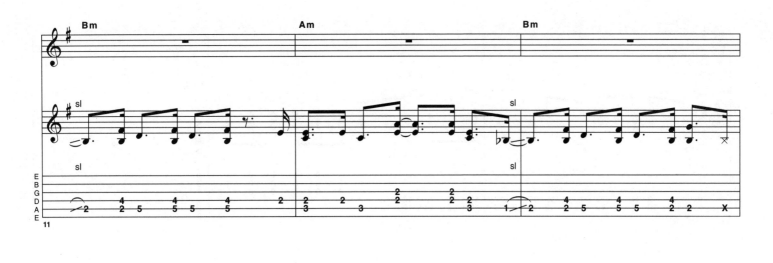

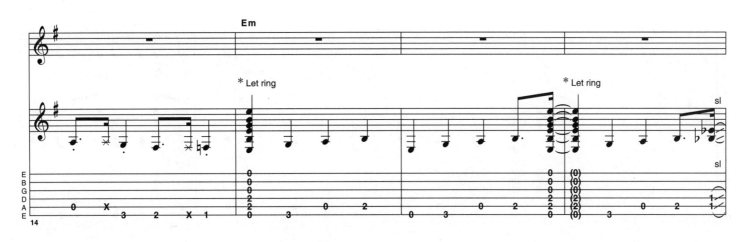

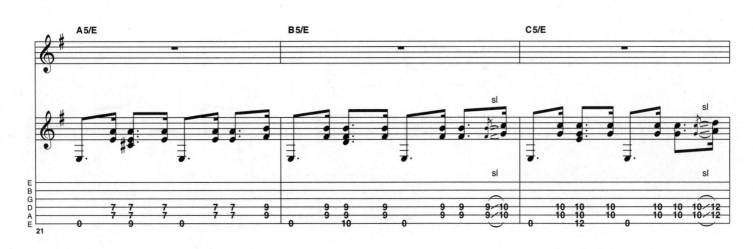

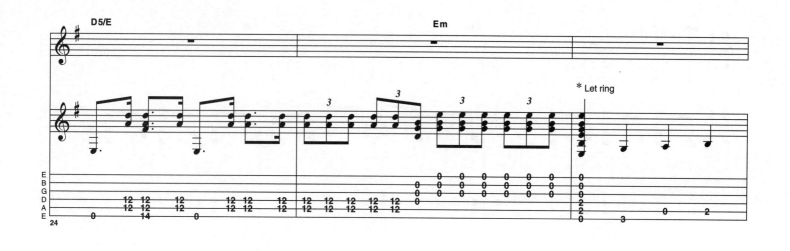

Well there's rock - a - bill - y cats, with their

pumps real high, wear - ing black drape coats, all real gone— guys.— And

cool skin heads with the rolled up— jeans,— look - in' real tough, and

might-y lean,— there's— a rum - ble in Bright - on to - night.— Ring—

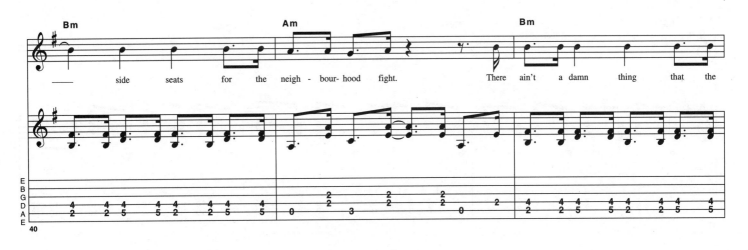

— side seats for the neigh - bour- hood fight. There ain't a damn thing that the

cops can do,— there's a rum - ble in Bright - on to - night.

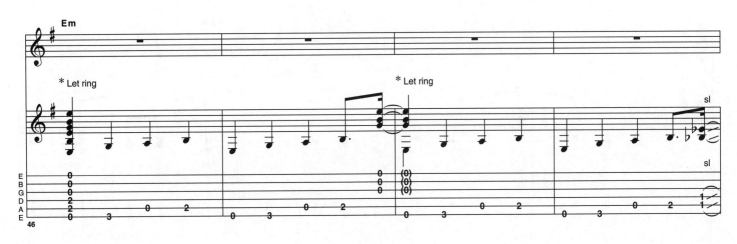

* Let ring   * Let ring

They— sew fish hooks un - der their

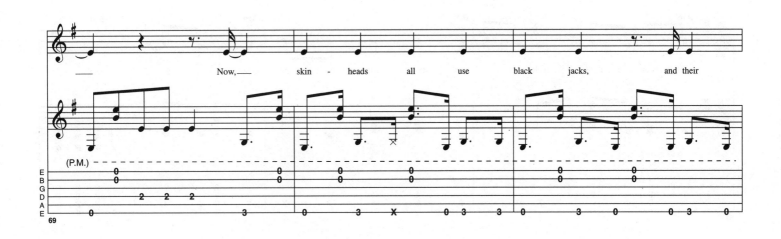

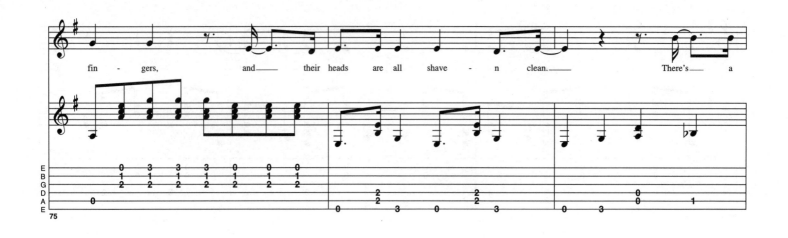

fin - gers, and—— their heads are all shave - n clean.—— There's —— a

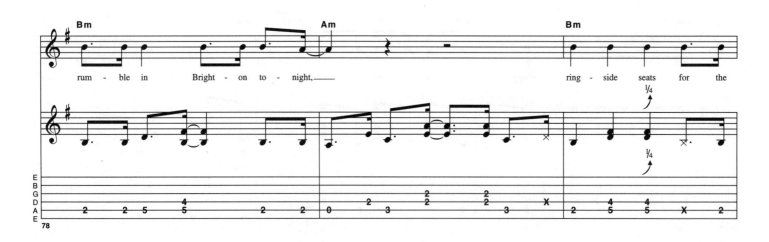

rum - ble in Bright - on to - night,—— ring - side seats for the

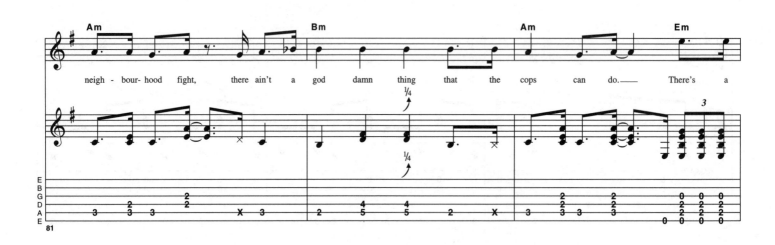

neigh - bour- hood fight, there ain't a god damn thing that the cops can do.—— There's a

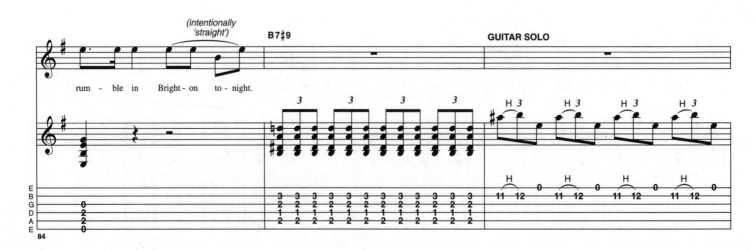

rum - ble in Bright - on to - night.

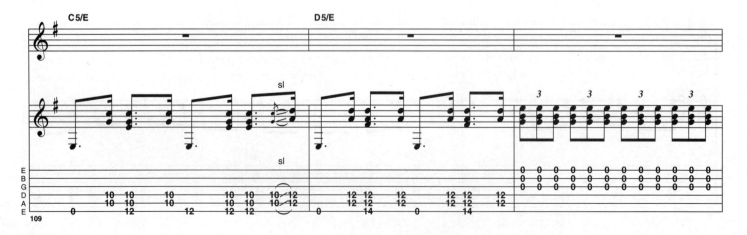

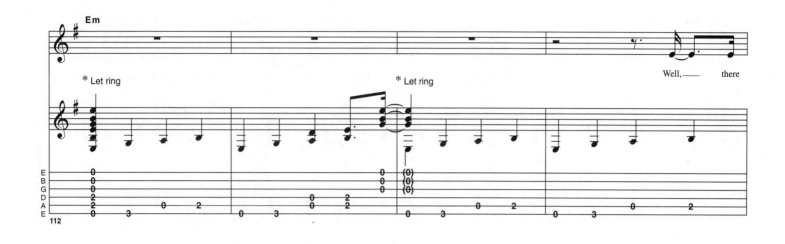

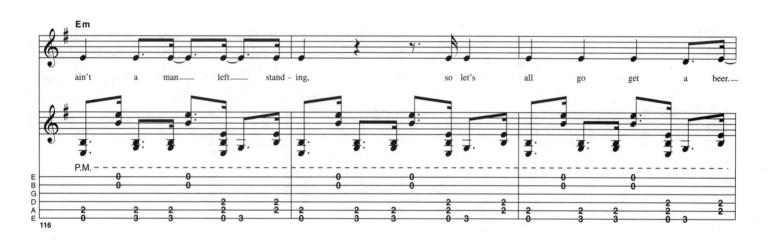

* pull strings
with one finger

Fishnet Stockings

Words and Music by BRIAN SETZER

Well, my sweet ba - by wears fish - net stock - ings, ___

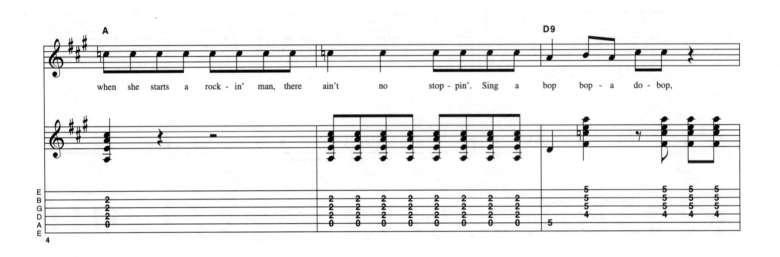

when she starts a rock - in' man, there ain't no stop - pin'. Sing a bop bop - a do - bop,

fish - net stock - ings, ___ shoo wop - a do - bop, when she's a rock - in',

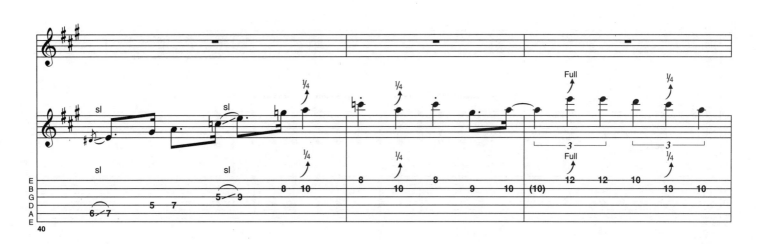

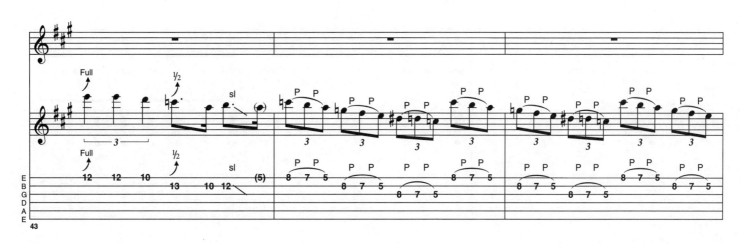

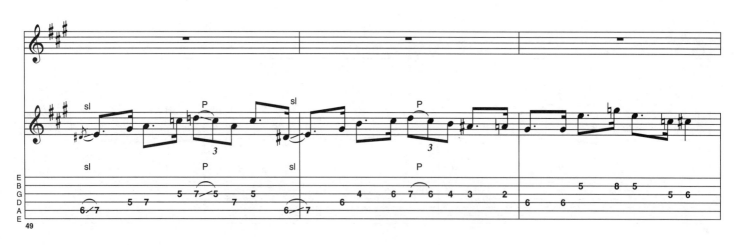

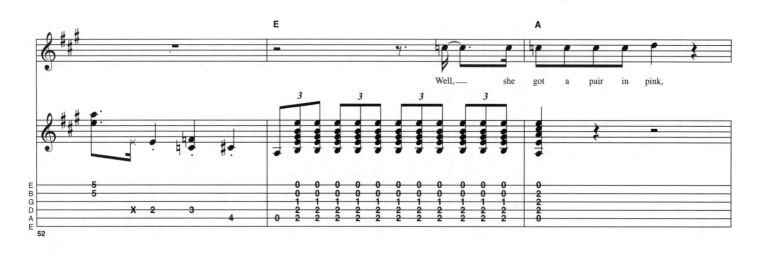

Well,— she got a pair in pink,

got a pair in red, when she puts the black ones on, she makes me lose my head. Sing a

Double-Talkin' Baby

Words and Music by DANNY WOLFE

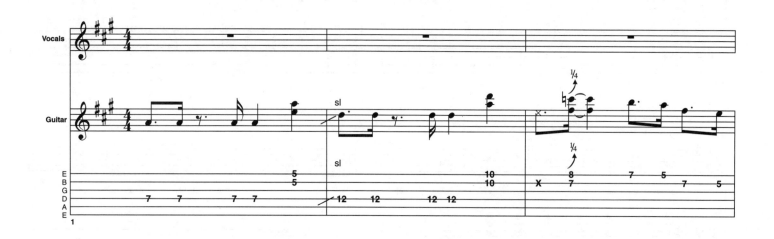

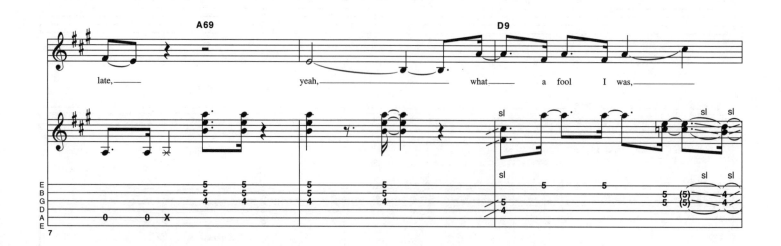

GUITAR SOLO

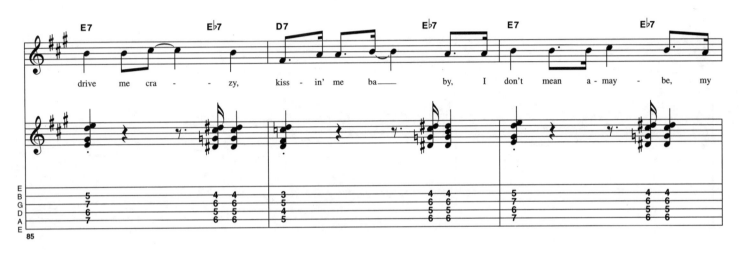

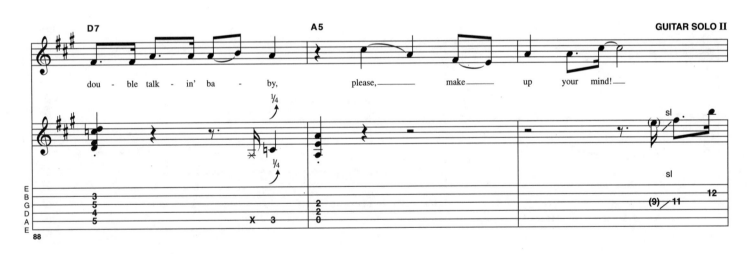

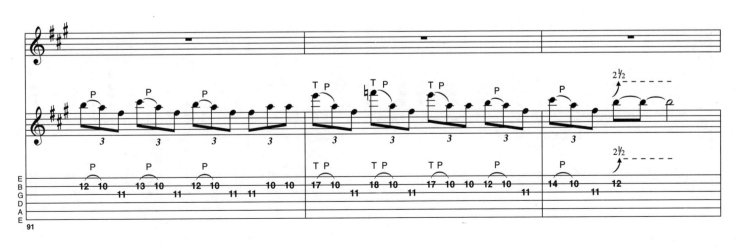

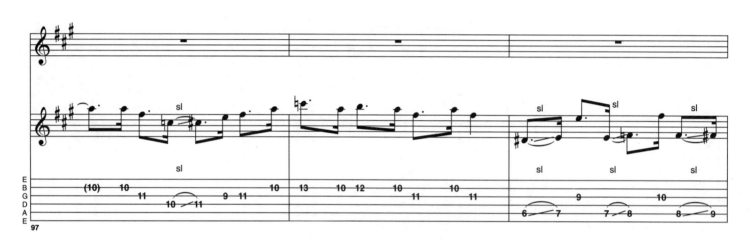

A69

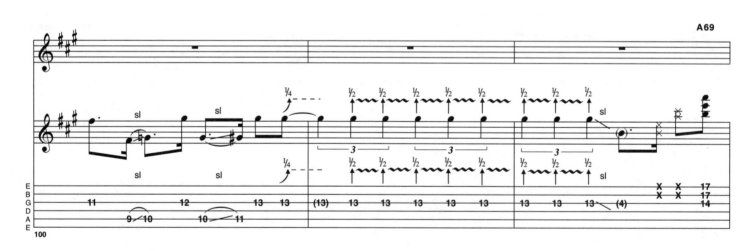

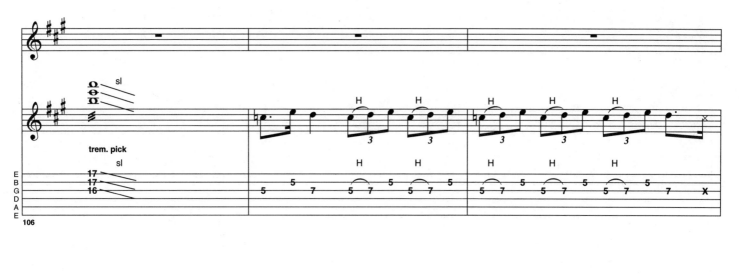

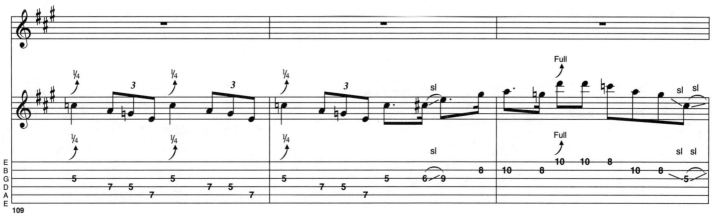

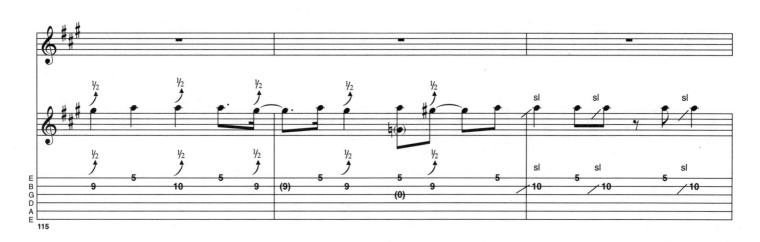

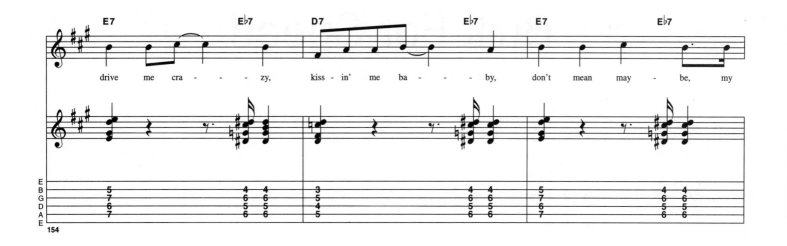

drive me cra - - - zy, kiss - in' me ba - - by, don't mean may - be, my

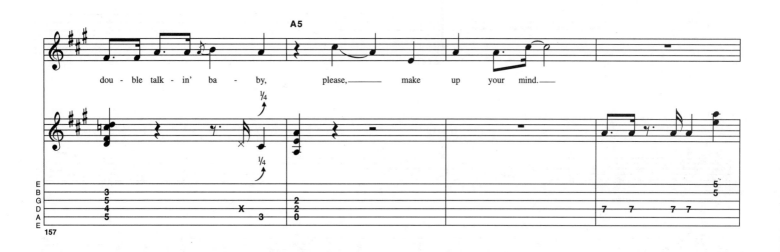

dou - ble talk - in' ba - by, please, —— make up your mind. ——

Yeah. ——

Built For Speed

Words and Music by BRIAN SETZER

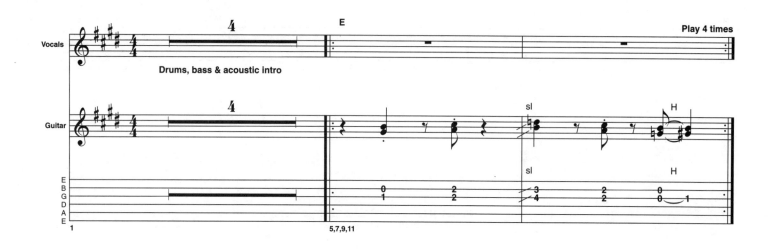

Drums, bass & acoustic intro

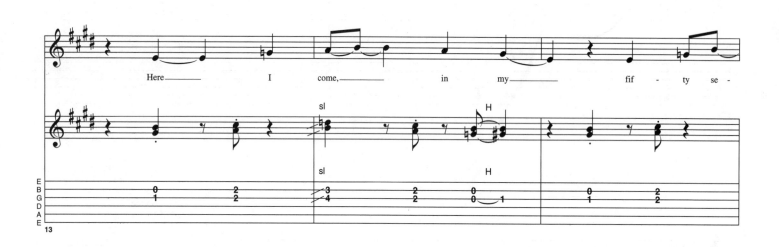

Here   I come,   in my   fif - ty se -

- ven, she's a real low ri - der,

ooh, _____ a - hoo hoo.

Vee _____ eight _____ en - gine, with a fuel _____ in -

jec - tion, _____ two, eight, three, that's my

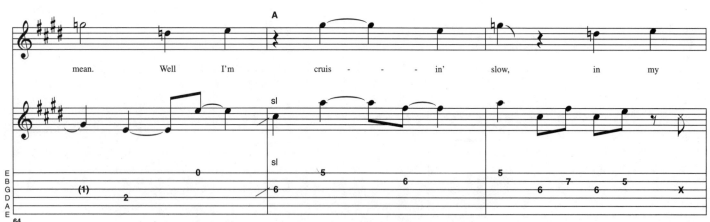

94

When I reach that fin - al des - ti - na -

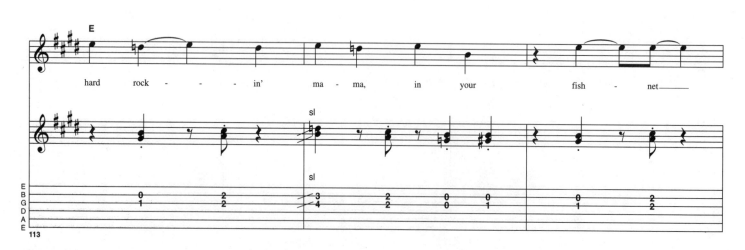

Printed by
Halstan & Co. Ltd., Amersham, Bucks., England

THE NEW BEST OF FOR GUITAR

Guitar Tablature

- The New Best Of series presents novices with an ideal way to capture the guitar style of their favourite bands at an affordable price.

- The Easy Tab Deluxe format is based directly on the authentic recorded guitar parts, simplified to make them easily accessible to beginning guitarists.

- The series contains some of the greatest tracks by many of the world's top classic and contemporary recording artists.

- All songs feature easy guitar tablature arrangements plus melody line, lyrics and guitar chord boxes.

- Every book contains 12 songs - excellent value at just £8.95 each!

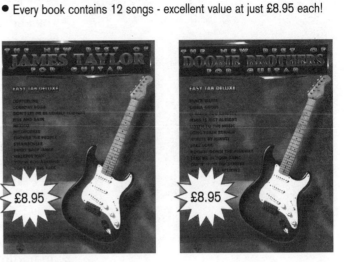

£8.95 £8.95 £8.95 £8.95

America   **NEW!**   Ref: 5692A
Includes: A Horse With No Name ● Daisy Jane ● Ventura Highway ● Sandman ● Lonely People ● I Need You ● Muskrat Love.

Beach Boys   Ref: 3443A
Includes: California Girls ● God Only Knows ● Good Vibrations ● Wouldn't It Be Nice ● Help Me Rhonda ● I Get Around.

Black Crowes   Ref: 5008A
Includes: Hard To Handle ● Sting Me ● A Conspiracy ● Remedy ● Hotel Illness ● Sometimes Salvation ● Wiser Time.

Collective Soul   Ref: 5009A
Includes: Bleed ● Breathe ● December ● Gel ● Sister Don't Cry ● Smashing Young Man ● Shine ● Heaven's Already Here.

Country Ballads   Ref: 4238A
Includes: The Dance ● I Still Believe In You ● I Will Always Love You ● In This Life ● Something In Red ● A Bad Goodbye.

Creedence Clearwater Revival   Ref: 3075A
Includes: Bad Moon Rising ● Down On The Corner ● Fortunate Son ● Proud Mary ● Susie-Q ● Born On The Bayou.

Jim Croce   Ref: 4455A
Includes: Bad Bad Leroy Brown ● I Got A Name ● Photographs And Memories ● Time In A Bottle ● These Dreams.

Sheryl Crow   **NEW!**   Ref: 0067B
Includes: All I Wanna Do ● If It Makes You Happy ● Strong Enough ● Everyday Is A Winding Road ● A Change ● Run Baby Run.

Doobie Brothers   **NEW!**   Ref: 5530A
Includes: Black Water ● China Grove ● Listen To The Music ● Long Train Runnin' ● Real Love ● Minute By Minute.

Doors   Ref: 3204A
Includes: Break On Through ● L.A. Woman ● Light My Fire ● People Are Strange ● Riders On The Storm ● Touch Me.

Eagles   Ref: 3136A
Includes: Desperado ● Hotel California ● Lyin' Eyes ● New Kid In Town ● Take It To The Limit ● Life In The Fast Lane.

Melissa Etheridge   **NEW!**   Ref: 5353A
Includes: Brave And Crazy ● Come To My Window ● If I Wanted To ● 2001 ● An Unusual Kiss ● Bring Me Some Water.

Gin Blossoms   Ref: 4650A
Includes: Allison Road ● Follow You Down ● Found Out About You ● Hey Jealousy ● Virginia ● 'Til I Hear It From You.

Grateful Dead   Ref: 4030A
Includes: Black Peter ● Box Of Rain ● Casey Jones ● Friend Of The Devil ● Ripple ● Truckin' ● Uncle John's Band.

Green Day   Ref: 4233A
Includes: Basket Case ● Geek Stink Breath ● Longview ● Stuck With Me ● When I Come Around ● Chump ● Panic Song.

Led Zeppelin   Ref: 3890A
Includes: Black Dog ● Dazed And Confused ● Immigrant Song ● Rock And Roll ● Stairway To Heaven ● Whole Lotta Love.

'90s Country   Ref: 4239A
Includes: Chattahoochee ● No Time To Kill ● Papa Loved Mama ● Put Yourself In My Shoes ● Red Strokes ● Fast As You.

Pantera   **NEW!**   Ref: 0052B
Includes: Cowboys From Hell ● 5 Minutes Alone ● Heresy ● I'm Broken ● Suicide Note Pt. 1 ● Walk ● Becoming ● This Love.

Tom Petty   Ref: 4454A
Includes: American Girl ● Don't Come Around Here No More ● Free Fallin' ● Learning To Fly ● A Face In The Crowd.

Bruce Springsteen   Ref: 4632A
Includes: Born In The USA ● Born To Run ● Dancing In The Dark ● Hungry Heart ● I'm On Fire ● The River ● Thunder Road.

James Taylor   **NEW!**   Ref: 0029B
Includes: Fire And Rain ● Sweet Baby James ● You've Got a Friend ● Shower The People ● Country Road ● Mexico.

Van Halen   Ref: 3444A
Includes: Ain't Talkin' 'Bout Love ● Dance The Night Away ● Runnin' With The Devil ● Jump ● Panama ● Unchained.

Neil Young   Ref: 4234A
Includes: After The Goldrush ● Harvest Moon ● Heart Of Gold ● Like A Hurricane ● The Needle And The Damage Done.

ZZ Top   Ref: 5115A
Includes: Gimme All Your Lovin' ● La Grange ● Legs ● Rough Boy ● Sharp Dressed Man ● Sleeping Bag ● Tush ● TV Dinners.

The Essential GUITAR SERIES

£19.95

- *The Essential* series contains the most popular songs by the leading proponents of seven different musical genres.

- Each book features note-for-note guitar transcriptions including complete solos in both standard notation and tablature, plus all vocal parts.

- The series covers many of the most popular electric guitar styles, from country and blues to rock and industrial music.

- The included Guitar Tab Glossary illustrates all the techniques necessary to play each riff, lick, fill and solo accurately.

The Essential 100 Classic Rock Guitar Fakebook **Ref: 0002B**

Contains 100 songs, including: **Stairway To Heaven** (Led Zeppelin) • **Sharp Dressed Man** (ZZ Top) • **Light My Fire** (The Doors) • **When I Come Around** (Green Day) • **Long Train Runnin'** (Doobie Brothers) • **Wild Night** (Van Morrison) • **Maggie May** (Rod Stewart) • **Time Is Tight** (Booker T. And The MGs) • **Hotel California** (Eagles) • **Peter Gunn** (Duane Eddy) • **Heart Of Gold** (Neil Young) • **Run Baby Run** (Sheryl Crow) • **Spanish Fly** (Van Halen) • **American Girl** (Tom Petty) • **Casey Jones** (Grateful Dead) • **People Get Ready** (Curtis Mayfield) • **Summertime Blues** (Eddie Cochran) • **Sheena Is A Punk Rocker** (The Ramones) • **Hard To Handle** (Otis Redding).

£9.95

The Essential Alternative Guitar **Ref: 4780A**

15 songs, inc. **Everything Zen** (Bush) • **Somebody To Shove** (Soul Asylum) • **No Rain** (Blind Melon) • **Longview** (Green Day) • **Run-Around** (Blues Traveler) • **Three Little Pigs** (Green Jelly) • **Milquetoast** (Helmet) • **Gel** (Collective Soul).

The Essential Blues/Rock Guitar **Ref: 4781A**

13 songs, inc. **Hideaway** (Eric Clapton) • **Tin Pan Alley** (Stevie Ray Vaughan) • **La Grange** (ZZ Top) • **Born Under A Bad Sign** (Jimi Hendrix) • **Oh, Pretty Woman** (Gary Moore) • **Bad To The Bone** (George Thorogood) • **Cities Need Help** (Buddy Guy).

£9.95

£9.95

The Essential Classic Rock Guitar **Ref: 4970A**

20 songs, inc. **Sultans Of Swing** (Dire Straits) • **Eruption** (Van Halen) • **Whole Lotta Love** (Led Zeppelin) • **Cinnamon Girl** (Neil Young) • **Evil Ways** (Santana) • **Riders On The Storm** (Doors) • **Show Me The Way** (Peter Frampton) • **Aqualung** (Jethro Tull).

The Essential Country Guitar **Ref: 4968A**

15 songs, inc. **On The Road Again** (Willie Nelson) • **I Will Always Love You** (Dolly Parton) • **Red Strokes** (Garth Brooks) • **Fragile** (Nanci Griffith) • **State Of Mind** (Clint Black) • **Southern Grace** (Little Texas) • **Red Wing** (Asleep At The Wheel).

£9.95

£9.95

The Essential Industrial Guitar **Ref: 0003B**

17 songs, inc. **Cowboys From Hell** (Pantera) • **Milquetoast** (Helmet) • **Filth Pig** (Ministry) • **Electric Head Parts 1 & 2** (White Zombie) • **No Place To Hide** (Korn).

The Essential '90s Rock & Metal Guitar **Ref: 4969A**

13 songs, inc. **Runaway Train** (Soul Asylum) • **Hole Hearted** (Extreme) • **All I Wanna Do** (Sheryl Crow) • **Walk** (Pantera) • **Lie** (Dream Theater) • **A Conspiracy** (Black Crowes) • **Souls Of Black** (Testament) • **Only** (Anthrax).

£9.95

AVAILABLE FROM ALL GOOD MUSIC STORES

If you have difficulty finding these products contact Music Mail on: **Freephone: 0800 376 9100**

International Music Publications Limited
Southend Road, Woodford Green, Essex IG8 8HN, England